"The job of the poet is to feel something deeply, and to make us feel it too. Nancy Levin succeeds wonderfully in opening her heart and allowing all of us to share in its beat."

— Marianne Williamson, the #1 *New York Times* best-selling author of *A Return to Love*

"Nancy's poetry is powerful and evocative in its authenticity. Each verse brings the reader nearer to an intimate encounter with the vulnerable, evolving self. What a precious glimpse into the inner journey home."

— Joan Borysenko, Ph.D, the *New York Times* best-selling author of *Minding the Body, Mending the Mind*

"If words of the heart are music to the soul, then Writing for My Life...Reclaiming the Lost Pieces of Me is the music our souls have been waiting for! Through each intimate snapshot of her life, Nancy awakens our own life-memories of deep love, cherished hopes, and great fears—and the healing that begins with the last word of each page. Nancy's poetry reminds us of what our heart already knows—that love is the great healer of life, and the memories of our love hold the power to liberate our greatest gifts, for ourselves and the world. I love this book!"

— Gregg Braden, the *New York Times* best-selling author of *Fractal Time*

"My mentor, the poet Kenneth Koch, taught me that the language of poetry is a special and unique language. Its words are polished diamonds that evoke deep feelings and insights. Its words are more beautiful and evocative than the ordinary words of prose or conversation. In her marvelous and lyrical and deeply moving book, Writing for My Life...Reclaiming the Lost Pieces of Me, Nancy speaks directly to your heart and to your soul. Her words and thoughts are indeed the polished diamonds that remind you, that transform you, that move you. I really enjoyed and highly recommend this collection."

> — Brian L. Weiss, M.D., the *New York Times* best-selling author of *Many Lives, Many Masters*

"Evocative and deeply moving, Nancy's poetic works weave their way into the hidden tender recesses of your heart and beckon new life, redemption, forgiveness and understanding. There are few poets who remind me, equally, of the wrenching sadness and the fierce joy of being alive. Her words will leave an indelible mark on your soul."

> — Colette Baron-Reid, best-selling author of the *Map: Finding the Meaning and Magic in the Story of Your Life*

"From the moment I first heard Nancy's poetry I knew she had a gift. Her words touch the heart of those courageous enough to set out on a journey of self-discovery seeking emotional freedom, wholeness, and a deep engagement in life. Sit back, let these words flow through you, and feel the magic of healing and aliveness contained in the pages of this book."

> — Cheryl Richardson, the *New York Times* best-selling author of *Take Time for Your Life*

WRITING FOR MY LIFE...
Reclaiming the Lost Pieces of Me

A Poetic Journey

Nancy Levin

BALBOA
PRESS

A DIVISION OF HAY HOUSE

Cover photo by Sharon Brender.

Balboa Press books may be ordered through booksellers or by contacting:

Balboa Press
A Division of Hay House
1663 Liberty Drive
Bloomington, IN 47403
www.balboapress.com
1-(877) 407-4847

ISBN: 978-1-4525-3223-3 (sc)
ISBN: 978-1-4525-3224-0 (e)

Printed in the United States of America

Balboa Press rev. date: 3/06/2012

a note to the reader

This book was first published in January 2011. It was, and is, a collection of poems. But since the first edition, I've discovered that it is actually more than just a book of poetry, more than just my own story on a page. It is a bridge. From my own experience to that of so many others.

Mine is not a solo story. I have read these poems before audiences of four to four thousand. I have heard from people of all ages and circumstances – those who have loved poetry and those who never understood it – that they find themselves and their lives reflected, revealed, through my words.

Writing is how I solve and dissolve complex equations of heart and head. It is my personal commitment to revealing, as poetry has the ability to connect us to one another. We discover ourselves in words, unveiled and immersed in the precision of the present moment.

I have been writing to capture and process the details of my life since I was 11, in seventy-five volumes of personal journal. Out of these pages my poems emerge, mined from the mosaic of memory, fragments of language, introspection and observation. The practice of poetry is my wayfinding. It's my guide. Distilling and illuminating the essence of a fixed moment in time, like a snapshot. The pure, concise extraction of an experience, like espresso. In some way, it didn't happen if I didn't write about it.

These are "my" poems, but not only mine. My story, but yours, too. A portal into the story of awakening. Internal wrestling. Self-awareness. Ending an 18-year marriage. And the freedom that came thereafter. Making myself vulnerable through these words has opened my eyes to the ways in which each of our stories are intertwined, coursing through one another. It's not only the meaning, more the feeling that resonates between us. We are all of us writing for our lives.

This newly revised and updated edition is divided into three sections, each corresponding to one of the stages of reclaiming myself. Here you will find the poems, and the context, that became the stepping-stones along my journey from fear to self-love and self-forgiveness. I offer my heart to you with the hope that it serves as a compass to lead you back to yourself, and an invitation to find and trust your own voice.

Nancy Levin
Boulder, Colorado
February 2012

over the phone
my mother says to me
you haven't told anyone –
i mean – you're not going to **write** *about it are you*

pieces of me

WRITING FOR MY LIFE...
Reclaiming the Lost Pieces of Me

A Poetic Journey

bone

For most of my life, I needed validation. I looked outward for permission. Permission to offer myself love and acceptance. I put everyone else's dreams and needs before mine. I spent my days managing the perceptions of others, projecting an image of perfection. In the process, I forgot something.

I forgot to live my own life.

I didn't feel loved for who I was – especially not in my marriage – so I believed I never would be. I checked out. Went to sleep. And was awakened only by an explosion of epic proportions.

After the dust settled, I had a choice. I could either stay numb and go back to sleep. Or, I could face my fears. I could embrace change. I could stop living my life in reaction to others.

And so the journey began.

The journey to knowing, deep in my essence, that I am loved. No matter what I do or don't do. Even if I don't do *anything* I will be loved.

But how? I needed courage. I found it in my body.

My body – flesh and bone – a treasure chest. Its cellular secrets under lock and key until the moment they were ready to be freed. The thaw came that way: an instant, a window, an opening. If I'd left sooner, I would not have been able to stay away. If I'd stayed a moment longer, it would have been radical self-betrayal.

I remember leaving for the last time. I bought a clean, new mattress just days before, knowing it was a last offering to a lost time. I quietly told the truth to someone safe. There was the night I thought I heard him coming for me – first hope, then fear, then resignation. I remember finally asking for help. I remember when I didn't think all the help was going to help. I remember when it finally did. I remember all the hours around the hours. Those hours building the skeleton of a leaving. Those hours of bone.

reclaiming the lost pieces of me

in seven hours
we reached the desert
by morning
clear blue sky
and red rock wake us
move us
remove us from
the usual

we travel
to see what happens
elsewhere
to find the difference
in ourselves
inside another place
reordering the regular
giving order to what has gone before

call for what has passed
and what will come
mark this moment

my body goes back
into the healing
it sits
in a canyon
i never left
drops down into
unlimited time

this writing
this ancient meaning of movement
distracts the body

creates a space
for the silence
of making

yes
each day
i can do
one more thing

seven river crossings
bridge past to present
rising and falling
between breath and bone
the perfect landmark
lights up a landscape

i could only come from center
something to go back to
so rooted and close to earth
becoming whole is a profound secret

each day – let go
everything is at stake ♥

volcanoes

we were born
into a mourning family
perhaps there are traces

i was born while they
awaited his death
could do no wrong
in space and time
since i was healthy

they waited
until he was gone
through kings and
wars and
volcanoes
to have another
traces that tell all

as we made our way
she was born
in the aftermath
invisible traces
through the universe

i was
not always
the oldest
child

i was
even though
no longer
the snow
even the healthy
melt overnight

my brother has died
perhaps there are traces
mother turned away
leaving behind religion
while in space
and time
father became more devout

as they make
their way
i side with my mother
how can there be a god
through the universe
if my brother has died

traces that
believe strongly
in the spirit
of the dead
walking through
doorways
volcanoes
i've passed before
traces that tell all

and i still find myself
even though
looking for him
overnight
in dark corridors 🖤

in the eyes of others

i
walking with dad
by the hand
by the pond
to feed the ducks

lots of black
curly hair
maybe i was five
in the little blue dress
with the sailboat
on it

he took me there
where it was full
of quiet and
crying and
flowers
he took me to visit
my brother

and that is where
and when
i came to understand
that i would never
be whole
complete
or enough
while so much of me
was underground
while so much of me
was removed

moved from family
to home
to garden
where
dead
jewish
children
bloom

he is my dormant side
who wakes
when i lie on the grass
beside him
as i wait for him
to come to me
to come for me
in the eyes
of others

ii
the picture i want
is of you and me
from years ago
years before
you consumed me

i do not remember
before
you left me alone
with them
before you took
so much of me away
before i knew i wanted to go
all the way with you

as it stands today
the picture is of only me
searching

it is only half there
i have always only been
half there
and aware of carrying
the burden of your death
of being son as well as
daughter

the picture i see
is of how i still
love you
once ago 🖤

band of gold in the bag

i remember
a story
you once
told me
of looking down
at your hand
one day
and noticing
a wedding ring
around your finger
with no recollection
of receiving it
until he came home
and asked where
supper was
and when
it kicked in
you knew
you must leave

so now
while
we sit
at a counter
surrounded
by coffee
that cooked
too long
and sat
even longer
in the open air
your drink becomes
increasingly weaker
by your eyes

and soon
you are
yearning for
the ocean

as you slide on the sand
you dream of burying the ring
but it will not come off
and when you wake
there are no waves and
no blue coffee
just a cold kitchen
to soothe your spirits

as you rise to do the dishes
you look down at your hand
and the ring is gone

late that night
you sit sipping some
hot tea and in the cup
you notice your
band of gold in the bag
and finally see
just how trapped
you will continue to be 🖤

we just have different maps to get there

light and mystery
curve
inside
the mountain
where we stand open
to the sun
at its highest point

the fatal mistake was in the punishing
the wanting competition for pain
the realization that
there must be something deeply wrong with me
to stay here with you

but if i had changed
it would have upset the status quo
it would have stopped transformation
from happening

the piece of asking for what i want
while giving direction
without fear of how it's landing
letting go of all
colors taste sounds

when i reach relationship
the samurai will no longer search
for how to serve

and i am untethered

freedom now
from what held me
hostage
the infidelity to myself

we will stay connected
by my accepting emptiness
give yourself an alternate choice
resurrection is imminent
we just have different maps to get there 🖤

listening for the one who cares

this morning
running up flagstaff mountain
i actually thought
i saw the ocean
off to the left
a distant mirage of
unconsciousness and
uncertainty
in this land-locked state

after a double-take
i realized how this custom
of leaving myself
lands and lodges in my core
still learning not to
muscle my way through what works
just engaging out of habit
now knowing it's the subtle adjustments
that make the most impact

on my descent
a baby deer was waiting for me
we locked eyes and
he let me get quite close
who are you i said
tears rolling down my cheeks

he can sense
everything i feel
i know his pain
yet cannot save him

in these moments
nature is the chime
sounding the end of
meditation practice
to wake me up
in the present

but i am not
a nature poet
so i don't know which
metaphors to use

most mornings i wake
while everyone else is still sleeping
and allow myself to think of him
as the sky slowly brightens
the land is still dark
trees in silhouette
against the early morning sky
i send him love and light

it is really only
ever about
time of day
and the passage
of night

but i am not a nature poet
though as we cross country
the horizon
a portal
opening up
right in front of us
port of *entry*
transforms into
po   e try

an adjustment period
coast to coast
this portrait of real personal markings
soft brushed color
deckled edges and draping
hide the cracking

i notice my past
pulling away from me
while i watch it in reverse
in the rearview mirror
cairns tracing the trail
from my ribcage
through my navel
to my pelvis
signaling where
the relationship
of one thing to another
ends

when someone goes
passes
from outside to inside
the heart
must adjust to the weight

why is it
we only have language for grief
over the loss of the dead
but not for the loss
of those still living 🖤

the warmth and the weight of you

the warmth and the weight of you
has stayed beside me
on the bed
the trail
the place you still occupy
the space still breathes of you
of your pawprint
imprinted on my heart

the deafening silence after so much laboring
going for the car
everyone said we'd know when it was time

i hear my bones whispering to me
you saved him – you already saved him
now go turn on the light
i must want life more than comfort
in any given moment

in my openness and acceptance
i willingly surrendered
my own sense of self
grateful for what was good
but i cannot do anymore than
i am doing already
there is no longer room for me here

you were the anchor
grounding us
keeping us together
our life was outlined by you
and then
putting a marriage to sleep by your side

what if the truth
about the destruction
is that we have been
suffering   drowning   suffocating
for as long as we can remember

the nevers pool and collect in my palms
tan lines of a wedding band removed
i'm going to hold you
hand over heart
through the wanting to go back

her voice in my head
it's just another contraction
the birthing process and dying are one

what if
getting out
is as simple as
going in

reconciling sin

whether you know it
or not
you have a tell
if you try and hide it
he will find it
but perhaps
if you live with it
integrate it
forgive it
accept it
use it
there will be nothing
left to find

i pulled the pin
yet it took nearly a decade
for the grenade to detonate
i was always lulled by
the rhythmic ticking
sometimes quiet
sometimes deafening
sometimes comforting
sometimes excruciating

no one seemed to see
it was a time bomb
from the beginning
that could never
be sustained

this man couldn't recover
from the experience of
being inside a woman
and then comparing it
to another man's experience
of being inside her

by focusing only
on the unchanged moments
instead of forgiveness and forward
only the piercing and the staying
the banishing and the beckoning
the punishing and the returning

and then
i vanished 🖤

on the threshold of something new

this is the summer
of heart ache and
goodbye

i wake and lay in bed
remembering all the things
that will never happen
all the places we will not go
all the things we will not do

the taste in my mouth
is of a marriage crashing

healing the past
inside the present
remains and relics
embedded and intact
a return and forward
an arrival

left alone in the dark
we each must discover
our own light

the hope is killing me
fear of being abandoned
for any sort of weakness
or not knowing
what do you think you've done
with all your feeling all this time

this gets you in trouble
interfering with decisions
already in progress
it's the fear that makes you question
not the faith
constantly recreating
the wounds of childhood
until they heal

seemingly stranded in the liminal
this time between
no longer married and
not yet divorced
on the threshold of something new

i made a promise that i cannot keep
it will shock you how much it never happened 🖤

into the uncertainty

last night
or very early this morning
he felt me awake
his deep exhale nestling
the nape of my neck
palm resting on the
small of my back
gently pressing down
to ground me

now
the shorthand
of a marriage
translated
over time
is a lost language
just ancient fragments
of letters and torn
corners of reverie

in the dark
as i move in bed
i get the sense that
i am too big for this
body i've had

i surrender and assign
the loving of my body
to you
until i am ready to
love it again

feel like i am pushing
myself out from the inside
stretching this restrictive
container

all the while
i cried and
she stayed
prayed with me
into the uncertainty
still she watches
clearing the way
while i cannot see
stands beside me
when i need strength
to move forward
gently reminding me
that it's always about
beginning
and then beginning
again

marriage
is a long time
to be away from myself 🖤

you can't be too careful

you can't be too careful about giving away love
keep a cache of withholding
so that you won't feel each pin prick
holding you like a specimen

at the end of the bed you may see
an animal begging for your heart
but you can't be too careful about giving it away

now the summer is penetrating you
illuminating what has been hibernating
returning ripe sensation to numb territories
but what you once loved
because you surrendered
still leaves a mark
forever etched and scratching 🖤

harbor

from this liminal state
we are reborn
into a threshold between worlds

through the fabric of fog
a map for another way
presents itself
we see – in a flash – how life could be

can we return to what is familiar
and make it new
finding mystery in comfort
or do i embark upon
the adventurous sensuous
on my own

surrender
to the acceleration of self-discovery
that can only come
from encouraging the emergence
of dormant forces

embracing this vantage point
let the past be memory

this pause
between present and future
is the alchemy
that will wake
unlock
transform

there is barely a moment
even in morning twilight
when i forget
to remember
the shift is happening

i am a light in the harbor
leaving the weight
of the past at sea
change is my anchor
deep inside
peace is so close 🖤

breath

I thought it was just about a marriage ending. But it was about so much more. Mourning the marriage, but also mourning the self I had been. Making room for the one I was becoming. That one – the new me – who could not go back. Who could not survive in such a dry climate.

Or could she? So much wanted to go back. How to hold that part of me? Simply hold it, and not act?

Uncertainty. The tension of opposites. How, just when we think we have landed, we are actually further unearthed. Ground must be restored, but not through stillness. Stillness will not satisfy. I discovered life as breath: fluidity is the only ground we can seek.

I remember the instant my marriage was over. Feeling like a failure for not fixing him. For not making the marriage work. For staying too long or not long enough. Waiting for him to sign the divorce papers. And also secretly wishing he would break down the door. Come back for me. How the jingling of any dog tags on any dog collar took my breath away. No idea that the last time I saw them would be the last time I saw them. Fun and happiness and pleasure were on hold indefinitely.

But then, a break. An unexpected encounter, a moment of awe. Sensation returning to my body. And there, my breath still held, I felt hunger for the first time.

And I cut my hair.

who and what is guiding me

this morning
as i am trying to leave the house
that robin is on my deck again
for the fourth day at my glass door
banging her beak
a beacon of restoration
and letting go

this spring brings renewal
for my mother and me

she assumed a personality much smaller
as a gift to you
in order for you to be a teacher of love
you would need to first feel unloved
something to resist
in order to find
the acceptance of yourself

perhaps i first taught her to love
perhaps i am now teaching her to love again too

where did this need to hide
myself
come from
in order to feel safe

don't ever assume
that the end of the storm
won't reveal the most exquisite sunrise
you have ever seen

we are forever
sewing together
scraps from dead bodies

a patchwork revealing the symmetry
between my fresh divorce and
my mother sacrificing her other child
in surrender all those years ago

now
just like her
it's my turn to
bury what i gave birth to

i know
i can no longer
stay with him
and although he will experience that
as me no longer loving him
it is the only way
we will each heal

you are being called upon to abandon your child
it will seem impossible
and it will be the most difficult thing you ever do
but you must choose your own life

but the fault line
inside me
has shifted
and the graces
are now scaffolding
on my own light 🖤

i am grateful for the breath in you

with each word
he shred my wedding dress
fifteen and
still eighteen years later
glass shards of language flying
stabbing and carving curses

now only white blood
sheds from tears
piercing and tearing
but he can't stain
my skin
anymore

what if the truth is
i should have left long ago
i mean
who does rebellion
really affect anyway

backpacking through
my separation
to find myself
on the brink of change
birthing a new past
while old is trying
to pull me back

the tempo of repetition
releasing into orbit
the spiral of non-linear time
folding in on itself
standing still

he gave me no solitude
and so we need
to proceed with over

one day
you will stop waking up at four am
one day
you will rise
and this will all have found its place
one day
i will have to squint in order to see
the scenes of that life i left

now knowing home
in myself
in my body

sensing that it is i
who will be
the brave one

and what if
this
is my body

the constellation
and the coordinates
tracking my body inside my body

one day soon
i will stand fully revealed
releasing the thickness
refining the muscles
this body defining me will return

and now a new voice says to me
whatever this is
wherever it goes
i am grateful for the breath in you 🖤

me, in the past tense

if mechanics is
the branch of applied mathematics
dealing with motion and
forces producing motion
then the mechanics of marriage
is the dangling limb of applied matrimony
dealing with fusion and
forces producing combustion

this fire died out
while no one was watching
and then no amount of
paper kindling matches or
the rubbing together of anything
could reignite was lost from
not tending while the wound
was still tender

and then
it's clear that some myths
are true

after months of burning
on the pyre of dissolution
combustible matter of the past
provide heat and light
forcing forward
inevitably
like that phoenix 🖤

at last

i breathe without thinking
wake without dreading
feel safe in my skin
after all these years of only sensing myself
like a phantom limb
at last i am here
love doesn't dissolve it self-corrects and
recalibrates over time
older now and with more accuracy
i trust 🖤

the wanting that is waking

i wake
gasping for air
i've been submerged
now finally released
repercussions repeating
cycles of measure
setting in motion
what will be
from what was
that part of me
close to death

each snapshot
a moment
in the mosaic of time
made of shards that
wear as they rasp against
each other
mismatched fragments
bonding along side
polished fluid contours

your brokenness cannot
be fixed by my truth

inside each thought is
a choice and
always another
memory makes her bed

the stitches need to be removed
lives unwoven
the pattern unraveled
setting consequence in motion
moving one time to meet another

today
the truth of silence
of alone is setting in
no more marriage

his voice
is just a distant rumble
echoing about
and from now on
there is no voice
inside my head
except my own

this morning
it's the wanting
that is waking
desire ripening and
rising inside
passion is roused
what lies beyond
is boundless 🖤

lean into the loving

my primary landscape
needs healing
crevasses and couloirs
reaching into spring
an initiation
way before this took root in me
the past unfreezing
echoing inside my present

theft continues but i gave it away
keep walking
and cleanse
watch for what needs to grow

i come from the canyon
left in the loss of the past
this primal concept
of giving and receiving
is ancestral
i took on his loss
by osmosis thru them
and the chasm was born right there
family legacy
picked up and carried forward

primary heartbreak is no longer
my marriage ending
it is only the breakthrough
to what i have been longing for

what we can't deal with
consciously
we deal with
unconsciously

you need a downstroke to ground
she said
if i was as powerful as you
i'd pay someone to stand on my chest too
this is the way that he loved me
containing me
restraining me
until i felt my own force

i brought myself here
i placed him there
had you ever believed you were enough
you would have left
i let him hold me until i knew freedom

my turn around is to know
i no longer need an empty well
to fill
reality is a rushing waterfall
a surge of relief invoking the truth
i can only know what i know
when i know it
i am the other half of this chaos
but still
you didn't break his heart
it was already broken

restrain relax surrender release
relieving myself from restriction
i now lean into the loving 💜

one breath is enough

one clear truth
changes the world
of illusion
at the speed of light

addiction regulates
perception and
this speed of change
tracks the cause
and effect of one thread
of choice

can't take
the speed of truth
so you take it
at the speed of a lie
slowing the realization

but one breath
is enough
to demagnetize
you

rituals of
unfinished business
consistenly renegotiate
the timing

addicted to my own
cartography
creating a field of chaos
guided by the compass
of my own curiosity

the pieces of memory
that i keep finding
in my pockets
of time twisting in on itself
retreating then advancing

thorns are holding them
together now
the cracking
and then back to black
before more cracking

but water runs
in one direction
only
what goes downstream
can never come back 🖤

immersing and emerging

i watch her swim
away from fear
toward a sea
free from restraint

she does not look up
or around
only within
breathing in and out
immersing and emerging

criticism crawls
out of her body
as she glides
into a confident sheath
peace ignites her core

for the first time
she understands awareness
by being seemingly unaware

standing now she rises
her flesh propelled by
bone   muscle   tendon
blood is rushing her
heart awake

all love begins
with self-love
once you know
you are the root
of your own suffering
choose to disengage
from the periphery

harness and recognize
the strength inside
to magnetize

breath is the private mantra
guiding prayer
follow your feet knees hips
belly heart hands
be willing to lose your balance
surrender to what matters most
and dive into the unknown 🖤

if we are not attentive, language takes the place of experiencing

perspective plays
in the way you frame it
objects appear smaller
or a memory fades
in the distance
how a hand looks stunted
how a life can halt
under water

the unwrapping of time
reveals the past and future
inside the present
there is as much fear in clinging
as in letting go

the point is not to stay
fixed in any role
but to be committed
to movement

we pass in and out
of one another
at every moment
you also have a body

i choose
to feel a heart beating
to know now instead of seeking separation
to focus on what is true not what is conjured

i long
to love without naming
to be immersed deeply not
disembodied and disengaged

the highest form of intimacy
does not have to annihilate difference
but we have driven the sacred out of it

returning from the mystery
into the world
the sense of death
is whispering behind us
all the time

as myth moves out
we have truly underestimated
who we are 🖤

Reconstruction of Desire

Within the canyon of my heart,
a dam is beginning to crack,
limits reached
by the pressure
of too much weight
finally exposing concealed weakness.

I sit, picking at the concrete barrier,
wishing for tools larger than
my own introspection and
aching finger tip.
This mosaic of
lost connections
is now my kaleidoscope
severing and reflecting
across this immutable boundary.

And yet I wait for the impact
of force and inertia,
the head-snapping,
breath-extinguishing seduction,
bargained for, yet elusive.
Ripped from the temporary condition
of being permanently interred,
fresh air filling my atrophied lungs,
finally speaking with my own voice.

Destruction restructures identity
a life of sign posts and
routes of travel
rutted by overuse,
impassable during the rainy season.
Acknowledgement of lost time
without which
nothing could now be as it is.

Confidence has staked her claim
atop the rubble.
The mask of uncertainty she once wore,
is now etched with the anticipation that
spring flora will emerge
from this wasted landscape,
adjusting to the healing discomfort
of debris settling.

What shall we burn,
send to the heavens,
let the wind vanquish,
tonght?

As Release and Surrender dance,
Chance and Risk wrestle
to rebuild the banks,
stirring us to cast our desire out,
reeling in the confident return of love. ♥

if i close my eyes the truth is familiar

the trick is
to find the silence
the stillness
the space between

tear away at the layers
i am a palimpsest
many lives erased
recollections seep through
what hides inside the quiet
the calm beneath the chaos

visions are often
accompanied
by murmurings
of the dead
let go
magic takes over
leaving the living
to pursue renewal

time is standing still
watching
lives on lives
beforeafter

knowing what you are
who you are
changes from moment to moment
from mind to eye to hand

the journey turned to history
most known and best loved

clarity comes from miles away
passion paints you
wraps you
awakens the imagination

truth must be discovered
moment to moment
a remembered truth
is a dead thing
it is the past
which links us
even in its absence
but it is the present
which we call our own
while the future looms
provokes and seduces

creativity from chaos
balanced around the heart
this body
is only a marker 🖤

i am the only one breathing inside my home

places of the past
haunt my memory
out of the corner of my eye
i am at once still walking those streets
while hovering above
observant on signs
that there's no place there
for me now
that is no place for me

today i sit with
whispers and visions
the present canceling past memory
altering future possibility

my spine is in a state
of being startled
central nervous system
realigning like a baby's
constantly pulling
myself back
to consciousness
there is a storm
on the surface
of the sun
i am reminded
of the emergency
reminded of how
i lost my breath and
voice before
and how my life now
forces me to feel

neither one of us had a
compass
a combination of maps
choices and fact finding
must teach us how to love
and be loved

at the trailhead
she said to me
you are the only one
thinking
inside your head
and now
mine is also
the only breath
i hear
inside my home 🖤

no now without then

there is a trick
no one tells
about letting go

you can't fully release
what isn't firmly in your grasp

everything we seek externally
must first be resolved internally

you must get right
to the heart of it
seduce the memories
immerse yourself in inquiry

truth will only
come for you once
embrace her and
she'll be quick
refuse and
she will linger

a tie to a certain time
will reveal a rip in the body
requiring remembrance
before being restored

goodnight to the way things were
sleepwalking through my unlived life
goodnight to the hiding
fear always finding a way to crush hope
goodnight to the woman i was
years of holding everything in

goodnight to the silence
my once strangled voice screams
knowing that no woman could stay
if i couldn't

seems like a long time ago – this
when i wasn't interested in time

but now the past is
burning away
and it has a distinct scent
which i've kept
to remind me
that what we got
is exactly what we needed
and that
i must be traveling

outlines and echoes fade
and by morning
all ocean and train outside
the pieces begin to re-pattern
extraction from the
quicksand of marriage
now embedding a new code
while preparing me
for everything
and this ♥

heart

Florence, Italy. In Michaelangelo's gallery, bodies birthing themselves from rough and ragged chunks of marble. "Unfinished Slaves," frozen in a state of self-excavation. I, too, was carving myself back into life.

Shame and guilt stripped away, revealing my raw flesh. I reclaimed time lost; my unlived life. Forgiveness arrived, tentatively at first. Then – now – in bursts of disbelief. Inhabiting my life completely– no hiding, truly living – is unparalleled.

Once there was a marriage and now there is me.

What do I know, now? I know that happiness, fun, pleasure – these are the necessities. I know that loss is loss and grief is grief. I know that forgiveness is the gateway; freedom and love lie beyond. I know that nothing is better than living my life as it is happening. Meeting the miraculous moments as me – just me. Just being me is the only thing I ever have to do to be loved.

I know that living on the other side of my greatest fear I can do anything.

On the next page is *hourglass: a last love poem*. The poem I wrote on the morning I finally filed for divorce. The poem that felt like an ending, but has proven to be a beginning. A kickstart, a catalyst. An invitation to a life I never knew was possible: this extraordinary life I am living now.

hourglass: a last love poem

i loved you
as much as i could
as long as i could
hard as i could
hard as it was

steadily holding on
to the small piece of maybe
that was finally destroyed

i have done all i can

we came together
in our respective corners
at the bottom of an hourglass
with our own strengths
our own wounds

marriage is to be found
in the voyage
through the tiny neck
of this timepiece

crossing up and over
to the opposite quadrants
those qualities of the other
missing in ourselves
are to be absorbed
for each to become whole

my love
hard as we tried
we simply did not make it
through the passage

the wounds too deep
the rage too loud
the voice too silent

and though i love you
i cannot be
married to you
i lost myself
in the giving of everything
to you

i now know
heartbreak in one
is a pain
unable to be healed
by the other

we can only
heal ourselves

for months
i have been nowhere
and everywhere
wheeling my home behind me
into the havens of others
now i need to land safely
inside the space of my own

i was starving to death
before hunger finally saved my life
waking me to desire

and now you are
free from the wanting more
than i could give
and i will love you
beyond the wound 🖤

what we exchange for safety

i am the holder
of your heart
the curator
of your memories
i was there
in the instant
that transformed us
transported us
transmuted us
and then
i couldn't hold on
any longer

there was a moment
before the books
were split
and the last of your things
left
when i sat on the floor
the next in a long lineage
of women
who had gone before

my breath arrested
in my chest
by the spellcasting
and belief
that everything has
only one answer

this all goes back
to the day we met
bypassing time
accelerating intimacy
blindsiding entwinement

but every power we animate
regulates the speed of realization
while one clear truth
dissolves the illusion
as we leave the whole false world
behind 🖤

what they don't tell you about love

he insisted upon everything being
clean and neat and showered and fresh
but what they don't tell you about love is
that there can't possibly be any chemistry
between disinfected bodies.
what they don't tell you about love is
precisely what i've come to learn about real love:
the messier it is the better.
boldly slap and harness the scent and taste of risk
as it bites digs drips swallows and rides us alive. ♥

being held and belonging

it all changed
the mood
the pulse
the pace
the swelling
the room itself
was swollen
grounded in trust
as if my body was a napkin
being pulled through a ring from the pelvis
deep into the earth

or like a candle melting down from the inside
dripping and pooling at the base of my spine
if i was someone who would say
it's my kundalini coiling and rising
then i would say that

now allowing my body
to feel the sensation of wanting
don't have to try so hard
don't have to try or think at all
to conjur anything to get myself anywhere
other than where i am

the point of contact
the point of entry
as friction gives way
purely physical response
riding the edge of the wave
unharnessed pleasure
blossoming and going over
the richness and

the yumminess of it
the heightened sense
of being held and belonging
upon return to this body and breath

let go of the ground that has held you
recognize that your only hope
is to be comfortable with uncertainty
so much strength and stamina
found in the ungrounding
sailing past safety

i can't go back into the darkness
after finally emerging into the light

finally
i am learning
how to be loved 🖤

the body remembers being loved

for ten years
the smell and the touch
and the taste of you
has been embroidered
on the inside of my skin
a still tactile reminder
each time i came up against myself
that i can indeed feel

the way your hand
down my spine
guides me
rising and falling
with breath and bone
i am leaning into you now

and in the exact right moment
your voice whispers

> *Keep your head up always.*
> *Your heart will struggle through this process,*
> *your knowledge about doing the right thing*
> *will at times falter.*
> *Do not be afraid to ask for help; from anyone.*

light floods the darkness
while pleasure escorts fear
pressing it into the past

for ten years
our real lives
have been
elsewhere

readjusting now through ritual
as old recreates into new

Believe in yourself and embrace the opening
of the french doors
into a beautiful new meadow
replete with the wildest wildflowers you can imagine.

our skin retains
the emotions of movement
the laying on of hands
a revisitation
into the silence
of memory
and release

And when you look over your shoulder
to see the distance you have traveled,
allow a smile to gently touch your face,
and taste the butterfly kiss of a new life.

the shell around my heart
that fossilized years ago
is finally softening
cracking wide open really
with the weight
of the wanting of you 🖤

breathed into life with a witness

for mollie and andrew, on the
occasion of their marriage

this passage, this private alter
is a ritual laced with wonder
you are one and you are many
coursing through each other
a layering, a peeling away
braided inside a single passion
in love, fear nothing

marriage is spiritual alchemy
the fusion of faith, a sanctuary
for insight reflection illumination

find freedom in partnership
blessings when solitary
compassion in truth
and always joy on your journey

surrender to the self-discovery
that can only come
from recognizing yourself
in another

so powerful to invite
this transformation
being breathed into life
with a witness

as myths fade
hearts open
eros welcomes wisdom
before you is an infinite coastline of mystery
into marriage--go deeply

when you lose yourself
you will find your way
inside the others' prayer

trust the
obstacles
to become
charms
it is the unknown
that invokes
movement
and resonates

marriage is a work of art
love is the movement we cling to
fingers tied into bows
bodies bouquets
while wedding bands embracing
can balance the earth ♥

they kissed us each goodbye

in memory of my grandparents
who died 20 hours apart

on the night
before my
grandfather
died
i sat with a man
i no longer knew
and in his eyes
i watched
night fall for
the last time

he wanted to go
for a walk
he told the nurse
but i know
he wanted to go
looking for her

there is
something
to be said
for love
everlasting
something
to be said
for lives
intertwined

something
to be said
for having
the sense
not to be
left behind

late that night
she came for him

i remember
waking up while
it was still dark
knowing that
one by one
together
they had kissed
us each goodbye 🖤

wellspring

i first walked inside your home
nine months ago
to begin the peeling away
and the healing

my whole life
has been leading
to a shattering like this
decoding the chaos
i created
to avoid the truth

water is a warning
words are heard
suffering is believed
walking comes hard

escape eludes and hides
but freedom reminds me
that the ocean cleanses
with each new tide
stripping debris while
depositing treasures
and that even the mountains
do not stay together

my soul knew
but i didn't want to see
so denial, she slows
the speed of growth

with each choice
power replenishes my voice
altering the relationship
between what is gathered
and dispersed

i return today
to your home
each of us a wellspring
inside the healing
and we begin anew 🖤

finish line

the way a sucker punch comes blind
around the bend
the way seeing both our names on a bill
still startles
the way canceling the number we had for nearly
eighteen years is a metaphor for death
the unsuspected blow of grieving the loss of a landline
by daybreak i am already broken for the day
breathing punctures silence
the finish line of marriage
a moving target 🖤

unbound

we may never know
how we hold
all we can
or how the light catches us
when we are out of breath

it's a sign of healing
to be feeling again

the real breakthrough
can only arise
from heartbreak

that which ails
cures
reminding us
that it's always about beginning
and then beginning again

as the waves crash me
i trust the sand
to polish my edges smooth
dissolving denial
revealing real
while courage and confidence
ignite my core

contraction and expansion
let the light stream in
and the stillness
after so much thrashing about
allows the body to wring
the sorrow out

as freedom floods
shadows may persist
know your undertow
as you alchemize the dark
and remember
that you always have
the strength to choose
how to engage

the clouds unveil the view
when you are ready to climb
now it's time to notice
the miraculous moments
in your life
as they are happening

this
is the making
of me
and we will walk
courageously
into daybreak
from the night
shining our light
together 🖤

imprint

as last night dissolves
into morning
as my belly breathes
into the small of your back
as our bodies imprint
each replacing
what has been displaced
i am now reassured how
mouthwatering it can be
to release my guard
stripped
in your arms' embrace
without armor
as lips and limbs magnetize
while sleep stirs
we are fluid and molten 🖤

restoration

the truth has been patiently walking beside me
periodically darting out in an attempt
to capture my attention
then today it just gently reached over
held my hand and gave it a squeeze
reminding me that i do want and need
and love

so this is what it feels like
to inhabit my body
a home familiar yet unrecognizable
breath hydrating the space
between flesh and bone

still flashes of the past hover
as film overlay on present day
haunting me with life before
and life unlived

once
i was a woman
with a husband
and a dog

it was a time
when water
didn't behave
as water

how quickly spells are cast
and broken
but life going on without me
leaves me breathless
so i trust in the power
of restoration

seems i am always settling in
and then settling in
all over again
to the changing terrain below
the weather is coming for us
and it's breathtaking

now loosening my grip
on what i desire
it draws toward me

what makes the heart
start beating again

balancing as i settle in once more

living and breathing
on the other side
of letting go

fierce
wild and free 🖤

terra firma

sifting back
through rack and ruin
from decades of debris
desire climbs
with each new
stretch of time
mileage
across ranges
seasons states and seas
now i am the woman
i have been waiting for 🤍

acknowledgements

On April 25, 2010, at dinner with Louise Hay, Reid Tracy and Cheryl Richardson, Louise asked me "What's next?" and before I could answer, Reid said, "I'll tell you what's next. You are going to read your poems before the Keynotes at our *I Can Do It!* conferences!" Cheryl and I both had tears in our eyes as I accepted the honor of his heartfelt offer – a fateful night indeed. The next thing I knew I was on stage sharing my poems with thousands of people, which led me to publish this book of poetry you are holding.

Cheryl Richardson: Thank you for being by my side every step of the way · a brilliant and brave midwife during the most difficult and painful contractions – and a beacon of light, love, strength and hope. Thank you for everything from endless hours of tea and writing in the roundroom to lots of lobster and champagne! And to Mikey and Poupon for letting me live with you the better part of last year, and for being family.

Louise Hay: Thank you for being my "Personalized Affirmation Action Figure," especially on the days where an email or call from you made all the difference. My friendship with you is one of the greatest gifts to emerge from my darkest time. *I am safe.*

Reid Tracy: Thank you for providing me with a platform for my poetry right along side my work in the world. I appreciate your love, support and understanding – and your heartfelt position each time you point out how happy and fun I am now!

Ibis Kaba: Thank you for being tough when I needed it, gentle when I asked, and for walking beside me on this journey.

Debbie Ford: Thank you for opening your heart and home to me instantly, and for guiding me through the darkness into the light. *The Shadow Process* was truly one of the most pivotal experiences of my life. And also, I thank you for being the keeper of my poems – my accountability to you of a poetry quota each week kept me right on track for this book.

David Smith: Thank you for being my trusted friend, protector, advisor, and big brother.

Maya Labos: Thank you for being my other mother, for always shooting straight from the hip, and for telling me to love my curves.

Rochelle Schwartz: Thank you for coaching me through twelve weeks of Spiritual Divorce, your direction – and love – was integral to my transition.

Mollie + Andrew Langer: Thank you for giving me the honor of writing and reading a poem during your wedding ceremony. Reid hearing that poem set all of this in motion. I continue to be deeply touched by our friendship.

Colette Baron-Reid: Thank you for being a dear friend and great cheerleader of my poetry, and for "bookending" your book *The Map: Finding the Magic and Meaning in the Story of Your Life* with two of my poems.

Bruce Kohl: Thank you for your true love of poetry, and for the perfect title.

Michelle Fox: Thank you for your friendship while providing me the courageous outlet for testing the waters with my poems in your blog *The Graceful Divorce.*

A deep echoing thank you to all the authors with whom I work · your words, teachings, and our time together have truly resonated with me and made a profound impact on my life. And an extra hug and kiss of gratitude to those of you who have specifically been right by my side, in friendship and support, loving me while I navigate my passage: Joan Borysenko, Gregg Braden, Barbara Carrellas, Wayne Dyer, Jean Haner, John Holland, Denise Linn, Lisa Fugard, Caroline Myss, Christiane Northrup, Doreen Virtue, Marianne Williamson, Brian Weiss.

Margarete Nielsen: Thank you for being my partner in crime, Hay Sister!

Balboa Press: Sandy Powell, Trina Lee, Lauren Allen, Andy Mays and Christian Kelly – thank you for your expert guidance, input, and resounding patience throughout our collaborative publishing process.

Laurie Halee: Thank you for taking me back in without missing a beat, and to Hank and Munch for welcoming me with open arms.

Kelly Notaras: Thank you for being the first friend I made in my new life – and a most surprising, exciting friend at that! And for introducing me to the mesmerizing Nicole Daedone and life-changing One Taste.

Jeff McClenahan: Thank you for trusting the spiral of time, and for lending your words to a few of these poems.

I offer deep gratitude to each of the following extraordinary people who've had a significant impact on my life, this past year in particular: Amy Hayes, David Bowen, Max Dilley, Laura Garnett, Patty Gift, Gail Gonzales, Ileen Maisel, Kate Moller, Jackie Rothstein, Robert Wilder, Bob Olson, Melissa Olson and Susannah Smith.

Janie + Steve Goldberg: Thank you for always giving me a home, and for being family.

Sharon Brender: Thank you for the fantastic photograph on the cover of this book! And to you and Mark for being family, too.

Patty Manwaring, David Gallegos and Patrick Kelly: Thank you for always trusting that no matter how far away from home I was, my heart was with you, and it still is. Thank you for helping make Boulder a safe, soft place to land again.

Kim Clary: Thank you for your openness and willingness; for holding me up when I could barely stand, for running with me when I could barely walk; and for boundless date nights at Café Aion.

Mom + Dad: Thank you for your unwavering patience, support and love. I am very grateful for the evolving path of trust, honesty and growth in our relationship.

Kate Levin Aks: Thank you for being my angel, fiercely protecting me and preserving me; for allowing me to take refuge in your home and your family; for sharing Allan, Isabel and Simon with me; for feeding me; for all your calls, texts and emails just to remind me of my awesomeness; for being here with me, and for me, when I needed you most.

index of poems

about the author

Nancy Levin received her MFA in Poetics from Naropa University. Since 2002, she has been the Event Director at Hay House, Inc. producing innovative events and experiential conferences around the themes of self-empowerment, healing and personal growth. Nancy weaves her poetry into keynotes, workshops and seminars. When she's not on an airplane, Nancy lives in Boulder, Colorado and you can visit her online at www.nancylevin.com.